YOSSI, YASSER,
& OTHER SOLDIERS

Jon Sebba

YOSSI, YASSER, & OTHER SOLDIERS

Winner of the
Utah State Poetry Society
Publication Award

Jon Sebba

Jon Sebba

Utah Poet of the Year 2013

Published by the
Utah State Poetry Society

To Roger
One heck of a big-hearted
friend. All the best.
Jon

Yossi, Yasser, & Other Soldiers

Printed by
ZDocs Printing
1084 E State Rd, American Fork, UT 84003

Cover Photo by:
Sfc. Al Chang, U.S. Army (public domain),
via Wikipedia Commons

Acknowledgements

This should be the longest section of this book, because we don't really exist other than in the minds of those who know us.

In my case, I received encouragement and help from members of numerous critique groups, within the Utah State Poetry Society, Arizona State Poetry Society, and other poets in San Diego and Redlands, CA.

I am grateful to many teachers including those of my early years: Yetta Sebba and Isador Cohen, and those more recent: Andrea Hollander (who helped by guiding me with an earlier version of this MS), Anne Wilson and Natasha Saje, among many.

I have warm feelings of gratitude towards Rita Bowles, Mikal Lofgren, Sue Ranglack, all the ScanCelts (Rose Ostler, Elaine Christensen, Kevin Clark, Orlan Owen, Anita Krotz, Lynne Benson, Lee and Ned Snell [and even Nancy], Keith Yorgason, the late Theda Bassett, Nad and Markay Brown, and all Three Sisters: Mary, Karen, and the late Helen); towards the pillars of UTSPS, including Clarence Socwell, Kolette Montague, Eric Read and LaVerna Johnson; members of Valley Winds led by Paul Ford III, and to Maurine Haltiner. Thanks and love to my children, David and Rafael Sebba, and David and Rysa Childress, and to all my UTSPS members, friends and neighbors for cheering me on.

Thank you to Carla Samore, who (with infant David) lived and shared the Six Day War with me – that seminal experience which forever changed us both.

I thank the UTSPS contest judge, Rob Carney. His appreciation of my poems represents an outstanding milestone in my life.

Gail Schimmelpfennig and Daphne Olsen helped bring this book to life. Thank you.

Last and mostly, I give loving thanks my wife Chris, who has for 28 years allowed me to focus on writing, encouraged and supported me through the manic highs and lows, and has functioned as my muse. Without her, this would not be. You have no idea.

Dedication

This, my first volume of poetry, I dedicate to those of all faiths, peoples and nations who have been killed or injured battling over Jerusalem during the last three millennia.

"Older men declare war. But it is youth that must fight and die."
— Herbert Clark Hoover (1874-1964)

"Never think that war, no matter how necessary, nor how justified, is not a crime. Ask the infantry and ask the dead."
— Ernest Hemingway (1899-1961)

FOREWORD -- Judge's Comments

I suppose some people think poetry's job is consolation. For example, we've been at war so far for most of this century; poetry should find, or make, or remind us of beauty beyond all that, especially since the news doesn't, or doesn't want to, or can't.

And I suppose others think poetry's job is confrontation. For example, we've been at war so far for most of this century, but you'd hardly know it; poetry should lever us off our complacency couches, should call us out for preferring lovely ways to go on ignoring.

Let's agree that poetry's job is both, and quite a bit more. Here's a book that knows that. It's not seeking or offering consolation, and it's not interested in confrontational posturing. I'd call the job it's doing - and doing impressively - reflection. Reflection, as in holding up a mirror to facts. Reflection, as in thinking vividly and long about sudden, horrifying, altering, unalterable, forever-lasting, unexplainable loss.

The power of these poems is that they don't explain. They present. What they present isn't pretty, isn't a jumping-off place for symbolizing or epiphany. And you should absolutely read them.

By read I mean experience. By them I mean truths about war.

– Rob Carney

Rob Carney has a BA in English from Pacific Lutheran University, an MFA in Creative Writing from Eastern Washington University, and a PhD from University of Louisiana-Lafayette. He is the author of three books and three chapbooks of poems, most recently *Story Problems* (Somondoco Press 2011) and *Home Appraisals* (Plan B Press 2012).

CONTENTS

FOREWORD – Judge's Comments

INTRODUCTION
    In Genesis /3
    War Poems /4

YOSSI'S WAR
    Mother's Diary Entries /7
    Someone Tries to Kill Me Twice /8
    The Wheat Field /9
    81-Millimeter Sentence /10
    81-Millimeter Reasons /11
    The Brume of Battle /12
    Clichéd Headlines /13
    In the Battle for Jerusalem /14
    Shell /16
    The Rider of the Red Horse /18
    The Truth about War /19
    Mud Coffee /20
    Forty-Five and Counting /22
    Footnote /23
    After Cease Fire /24

YASSER'S WAR
    Refuge /29
    Bystander /30
    Dirge /31
    Khirbe /32
    Wages of Innocence /34
    Embers /35
    Black Birds /36
    Nevé Shalom – Paths of Peace /37

OTHERS' WARS
      WWI – Glamorous War /41
      Assault at Normandy /42
      Why is it Dark at Three O'Clock
            and Why is Snow Falling? /43
      Poem with 25 Random Numbers /44
      Nailbiter /45
      Saffron Sage /46
      Phone Call /47
      Shame /48
      On the Road to Tehran /49
      Meat on Butcher Street /50
      Not Family /52
      Another Monument to War /54
      Nice Guys /56
      You Don't Know Scared /57
      Kandahar Haiku /58
      Grandpa Cries /59
      Mount Timpanogos Talks /60
      Desert Dreamer /61
      On the Lawns of the War Memorial /62
      Immortal Enough /63
      Daisies in Rifle Barrels /64

OTHER INFORMATION

INTRODUCTION

In Genesis

In Genesis
    the boy hauled the wood
    the man carried the flame and the knife.
    The son asked his father,
        Where's the ram?
    The father replied,
        God Himself will provide.

Now
    sons are trained to fight,
    they carry both fire and sword,
    they ask no questions
      of flag-waving fathers who send them off.
   No angelic voice cries out
      to stay the hand,
        no stand-in ram is found
          as the blade swings down.

War Poems

words can
ease trauma
make loss bearable
even resurrect the dead

but they cannot stop the slaughter

YOSSI'S WAR

Mother's Diary Entries

Jerusalem, May 22, 1967.
Risked our lives today. Took a taxi
to the Old City to see our daughter-in-law,
D'vorah and our newborn grandson.

The taxi squeezed through narrow streets
between gossiping hedges and hushed
dolomite walls to Montefiore's windmill.
From there our guide and driver showed
us *Gai Hinnom*, where he believed Canaanites

sacrificed their children. Rumors have it
that Nasser has blockaded Eilat, but who knows
what to believe. The cabbie, a goat of a man
in his fifties has a little beard. His two sons
have been mobilized, like our Jacob.

The whole country's worried that Egypt
will attack. Maybe Syria and Jordan too.
Look there, he pointed down through the haze.
We could just make out the Dead Sea, a sliver
of lapis fed by the Jordan, a vertical mile below.

The cabbie said the streets would soon be emptied
of young men and cars. We asked him to take us
to the airport tomorrow. After we leave, if Jerusalem
is bombed, he'll check up on D'vorah and the baby.
He'd telephone if he heard anything about Jacob.

Chicago, June 5, 1967.
War in Israel. I sit near the phone, knitting,
waiting out the night. When I can't knit anymore,
I write in my diary. And wait. And wait.

Someone Tries to Kill Me Twice

The skirling of ricocheting bullets
      seems
      to   come
           from   every-
                    where.

I dive down, till I'm flat as ground.
Unsure that I'm out of sight,
I press my lips to the dirt
like a khaki-clad ostrich,
tail visible along the ridge.

             Bullets
      snap. Stones

                crack.   From

                 where?

Cries.   Curses.   Shouts.

Fingers accuse a stone house.
Return fire. Then – silence. They escaped.
Medics check – relief. No wounded.

The second time, they use 81 mm mortars
from a mile away. They blind Motti, kill
Yossi and Mordi, and paralyze the radio man.
I don't care who's firing,
from where or how many.
I don't shout or curse.
I weep.

The Wheat Field

They cut and crawl over barbed wire
through the orchard of gnarled olive trees
into forty acres of summer wheat, slithering
on the furrows, faces, bellies and knees pressed
into the sandy soil, hidden
until the bristled grain burns.

A June breeze herds the smoke and flames
toward them. A storm of bullets rages above
the concealing dry stalks, pointing at the sky.
The heat and floating embers close in.
Their choices are as lousy as Sophie's:
lie there and suffocate –
stand up and die.

The soldiers roll, flatten the yellow hay
in the shapes of angels, pull up stalks
wherever their hands can reach,
empty canteens over their shirts,
cover mouths and noses.
The line of fire burns the field black and bare
until little remains, except acrid smoke
tinged with the smell of singed khaki, hair
and men exposed like ducks on a pond.

81-Millimeter Sentence

It travels only one way: from there to here.
Definitely not a straight line. The round is dropped
into the hollow tube. As it hits the base, it fires.
A **whump** vibrates the ground, shoots
the solid eighty one-millimeter cylinder, arcing ahead
of its aluminum tail, ensuring a looped flight
and head-down impact. Front-end charge
is primed and explodes on contact.
A body-violating **crash** craters bloody dirt.

To summarize:
two explosions shake the ground –
one there followed by one here.
The two punctuate a cogent sentence
in an aggressive argument, sadistic syntax
understood only by mortars and soldiers,

> (Whump) *I'm coming –*
> *to kill you* (crash).

81-Millimeter Reasons

On his mile-long arc, no one hears
81MM-No. 462307 musing:

It's good to be up and away –
heavy load, but great view.
Let's see … what's the flight plan?
Looks like … thataway, over there, between
that cluster crouching behind a low wall
and one in the foxhole; with a beard.

If I land next to that one
outside the wall, that'd really surprise him –
shoot gravel and shrapnel through
him at the speed of sound. A goner.
He'd hear me coming,
he'd never hear me hit.

On the other hand, I could crash
just inches to the left,
explode behind the wall.
That'd get a bunch of 'em
with steel splinters, stone shards.
More efficient. Yessir.
That's the way to go.

And he does.
He makes a bloody sieve
of the lieutenant, penetrates
Sammi's backpack radio to his spine,
blinds Peretz.
But he leaves the bearded soldier
in one piece, untouched in his foxhole
momentarily blind and deaf;
permanently riddled with guilt.

The Brume of Battle

When you find yourself in a cloud this thick
all escape routes disappear – you're lost.
This is not a mist or pea-soup fog near the shore
that blocks only the view. It's an oozing curtain
that infects your senses, thought and reason.

You hear noise, sounds too muffled
to grasp. This fog's wet with clammy sweat,
terror, the unseen. You blindly grope your way.
Fragile blood pulses in your ears, heartbeats
drum against your ribs. Ear-splitting blasts
all around, the loudest noises ever heard,
with screams and shouts from many quarters.

Whir of ricochets and chips of stone fly past,
your face flattens in dust, and the high whistling
whine of inbound shells descends the scale
before you're deaf and blind again;
until your senses return to tell you the good news.

What do you know? Who's shooting whom?
Where are you? Where are they?
Who's against you? Who's got your back?

Will you survive the next deafening thunderclap?
In this mire and muck, is there a God who knows?

Clichéd Headlines

It's War! I think, as olive trees explode nearby.
Tall pines, decapitated with a whistle and explosion,
trunks of others cut and shattered,
blown apart and scattered.

Artillery Rounds, a mere phrase in a newspaper
until the ground heaves with a deafening roar;
detonations follow our truck. Tight-packed,
we ride up Government Hill to cross the line.

My first corpse, an enemy boy.
Dead in His Tracks, lying nose-down
staring at cracks in asphalt. *Killed
in Action.* The phrases taunt me.

Our M-45 Pershing stands still – *Tank Kill* – marked
by one small hole. *Armor Piercing Round* pancaked
the crew inside the turret. I retch against the still warm
steel. *Reality of War* rakes my gut. I shiver.

Mortar Shells Rain. No, they don't – they roar.
I hack at a foxhole, body deep, to hide.
The shell-bursts drop clods of dry earth
down neck, push sand in mouth and nose.

A long whine; a short blast; three men
catch one behind the fence. Nathan's legs splinter,
Aaron is almost decapitated, and Danni so blown apart
they put pieces of him in plastic bags after the barrage.

I sink down, my back against a fractured olive stump –
chin on chest, arm on knee – no clichés; no words.

In the Battle for Jerusalem

cannons drown out pigeons cooing in olive trees.

Soldiers see death clearly. Their ears
are deaf to destruction. Cordite burns
the nose. The air is thick with dust
of rock lichen. Mordecai, Ahmad and more
die in *El Kuds*, The Holy Place.

A few doves may outlive the cannons.
Fathers die. Wives cry. Limestone outcrops
stand in meadows, bloodless in no-mans-land,
roches moutonnées[1], sheepish tombstones
in the battlefield.

After the lists of the dead exceed some
random number, the generals and gods
will be appeased, their bloodlust quenched.
But what about the next generation –
those orphans of the Angel of Death?

The demon's sword reflects the light
gleaming in the prime minister's eyes.
He sits high behind the lines, and talks
about collateral damage and strategies
to recapture the past
now in ruins.

Peace,
in a voice like Rachel's, weeps for her sons,
her eyes water in the smoke, her hair rinsed
in flame. She will burn olive branches
in *Gai Hinnom*[2] in memory
of souls sacrificed today.

---

1 *Roches moutonnées* (French) lit. sheep rocks – a rock formation eroded to scattered, sheep-sized blocks of white limestone.

2 *Gai Hinnom* (Arabic and Hebrew) lit. Valley of *Hinnom*, Joshua 5:18, – south of ancient Jerusalem, a place of fires, where Canaanites sacrificed their children to idols. To Jews, Moslems and Christians, *Gehenna* represents the fiery place where the wicked are punished after life.

Shell

I lie in a hole beneath bowed olive trees.
At arm's length, Yossi crouches behind
a marble figure, two millennia old.
We wait, alive but deathly quiet.

I think back two weeks. Politicians
were still posturing, war was rumored.
Thirteen days ago, we were mobilized.

Yossi came back from Europe.

On both sides of the border,
troops massed – them and us.
Yossi returned too late to be mobilized,
too embarrassed to stay indoors, he volunteered
in his Fiat, his own khaki shirt,
slacks and street shoes. He
tagged along with Company C.
He said, *They gave me no rifle,*
but a shovel for my troubles.

We dug trenches for others,
then rode a truck in silence
up Jerusalem's hills to the border.
Behind us, Yossi's Fiat followed.

Yesterday, June 5th, the battle began. Arabs
captured this hill. Company C drove them off.
Yossi with us, in his khaki shirt, still unarmed.

Last night, from afar we saw
the Dormition in flames. Paratroopers
fought Legionnaires. Cannons pounded.
Shooting-star flares burned, turned
the night white and the ground black.

Today, I lie flat in my trench. A yard away
Yossi crouches behind a Roman statue
in an ancient grove of olive trees
on a hill overlooking Jerusalem
waiting for the counterattack.

The wife and I just returned, I hear,
from a fertility clinic in Switzerland.
After eight childless years,
Laura's happy, he cheers softly,
inside her, a miracle's begun –
I'm a daddy!

Unheralded, a high-looping shell,
launched a mile away, spirals in
with a haunting whine,
shatters the statue,
olive tree, and Laura's dreams.

Randomness mocks me; chaos
and thunderclap stink of cordite.
Violence shocks the rocky ground.
Help me God, I pray in tears
face-to-face with the earth.

By his blood-soaked collar and belt,
we drag back a fragmented Yossi,
our shredded straw man
in his sitting-duck khakis,
broken shrapnel through his heart,
dead father of an unborn son –

another sacrifice on The Rock.
One more son of Abraham, bound
and trussed by duty,
slaughtered for The Land.

The Rider of the Red Horse

*And there came a blood red horse; and power
was given to her that sat thereon to take peace
from the earth ...*

— after Revelation 6:4

She climbs uphill through the smoke, from the direction
of the enemy lines, under the weight of a too-large drab-
green overcoat over a frayed gray sweatshirt. She shud-
ders. The June evening air wafts a burnt gunpowder stink
overhead. A soft gust flaps her coat against bony legs. The
collar gaps away from her neck to reveal her gaunt wind-
pipe with the clarity of a da Vinci pen and ink. In moon-
light, her skull is visible beneath her skin, translucent as
a lampshade in the Holocaust Museum. Her eyes cower
beneath cavernous brows. Taut sinews under her hollow
cheeks work her jaws. Her thin lips barely move. In the
trench, we lean closer to hear above the burst of mortars.
Veins in her neck pulse blue; pupils of her eyes glow black.
She turns aside, swirling ash. We glance at each other –
warning eyes wide with fear. By morning, she's seduced
four of our company.

The Truth About War

A snaking convoy of tanks and trucks halts at a destroyed bridge. Soldiers climb out. Two jeeps of the recon patrol start down an unpaved road, as if on a weekend outing. An explosion. We all dive under the trucks, not knowing the front jeep has hit a mine. When we look again, it's lying upside down like a tortoise flipped on its shell, roof crushed, wheels spinning in a cloud of dust.

The second recon jeep speeds forward to help friends pinned beneath the first. It too explodes – another landmine. After the echoes die, we can clearly hear the cries of the wounded. Mine-sweeping specialists are called. In slow motion they walk, swinging detectors side to side; more mines found and marked with little red flags.

Another jeep careening along our road from HQ screeches to a stop. A runner jumps out waving a wad of papers. We hear him shout, *Those are our mines – laid this morning. Here are the maps.*

Mud Coffee

Avi, really Avraham, and I crouched
on Commissioner's Hill watching the abbey
roof, wooden beams and shingles burn;
a Roman Candle for Independence Day.

I learned a lot about him sharing a foxhole:
his hopes, his taste for sweet Turkish "mud" coffee
sipped slowly at a sidewalk café on Magnes Square –
its thick grounds lingering on the tongue,

his love of genetics, his work at the orphanage,
repairing a modest home, and his wife, Tanya.
Then he crawled away, body pressed to the earth.
He took with him answers to my unasked questions:

Did he play chess? Music? Favorite books?
His parents? Did he and Tanya have children?
He disappeared when the shell exploded.
After the fighting, I searched the front,

the command bunker, the triage center.
He'd gone without even a *Goodbye, friend.*
I looked through the City, the orphanage,
the café in the square that served mud coffee.

He wasn't at the Biology Department, though
in his office, large boxes, labeled in large black letters,

"AVRAHAM FINE"

waited for him, as though he'd been laid off
but had forgotten to clear out his desk.
He wasn't at home in Talpiyot, where I found
Tanya crying in a darkened house.

One day, I'll return to Jerusalem,
to that café between the oaks
on Magnes Square. I'll sit and order
a demitasse of thick, gritty coffee.

I am sure that before I drain that thimble-cup,
before the taste of sweet "mud" leaves my tongue,
he'll stroll up, grab a chair, and call to the waiter,
I'll also have one – same as my friend.

Forty-Five and Counting

Yossi Levi died on June 5, 1967
Government Hill, Jerusalem

Yossi taught me several things:

He taught me   that virtue does not insure a long life
          and   after death the pull of gravity increases –
                 a dead body is heavier than you'd think;

          that   shrapnel punching through your friend's heart
                 can scar you for life
          and   the spectacle returns like shadows at dawn.

He taught me   that a war is no way to find peace, winning
                 doesn't evoke sympathy from your enemy
          and   losing is worse;

          that   killing people makes enemies of their brothers
          and   you can't count their sisters among your friends;

          that   in the absence of truth there is faith –
                 when faith weakens, there is memory
          but   even memory is unreliable.

 Yossi taught   that a man you knew for a few weeks
                 who died in a war of only six days
                 can be mourned for 45 years and counting;

          that   you may not remember whole years of your life
          but   try as you may you can't erase from memory
                 those thirty minutes of death.

Footnote

Lt. Col. Dreizin himself twice more wounded,
was down to ten men (from two reservist battalions).
— *Six Days of War*, Michael Oren, historian

On furlough, we stood wordless before Mordi's daughters
and Yaffa prostrate among mourner-women in black
ululating, Mid-Eastern style, tearing hair and crying.

With a thousand others, he died.

One thousand Mordis, one thousand widowed Yaffas;
many thousands of orphaned daughters and sons
and many more parents and friends.

He was only one – Mordecai, the plasterer. We called him
Mordi, husband of Yaffa, a teacher beautiful as her name.
Mordi, Morrocan immigrant. Mordi, father of Ahuva
and Ziva, daughters with teenage growing pains –
orbiting boys, pop music, peer opinion, chafing
against parental restraint.
Mordi, son of aging immigrant parents, struggling
with the new language, health care and pensions.

Mordi was only one of a thousand average, typical,
hard workers, stretched between shrinking means
and growing ambitions, declining energy
and increasing waistline, like many reservists.

With one thousand others, he died in that war.

Dear Mr. Historian,
Your record would be more faithful, had you dwelt less
on brave colonels, like Dreizin, and more on the Mordis
and their orphaned families, who didn't earn
even a footnote in your version of the War.

After Cease Fire

In August, our reserve unit is remobilized
to Bethlehem to guard prisoners. Untrained, we hate
being jailors of community leaders guilty
of protesting our occupation of their lands.

We accept a welcome break when we're ordered
to board trucks for a ride to the hill east of Jerusalem –
the same hill we'd captured in June. *To make a movie,*
our replacement lieutenant tells us, to re-enact the War.

In disbelief, we don battle fatigues and helmets again –
this time without Motti or Sammi, drive to the rusty coils
of razor wire, where we'd broken through before.
                                        That time
we had no wire cutters. A battalion of soldiers, pinned down
behind barbed wire, while someone was sent to HQ for pliers.
                                        This time
twisted strands reseal the gap. The movie crew rolls film
while we untwist new wires and run through without delay.
Pyrotechnics scream just as loudly though no one
wets his pants as we advance on the guardhouse,
its walls replastered. Special-effects people buried squibs
in the new patches which explode while we shoot blanks
in the direction of our friends inside playing Legionnaires.
The "enemy" fires back, though this time no one's killed
or even hurt. We run alongside a shiny new Centurion tank.

On June fifth, an armor-piercing round hit and destroyed
our old M-45 Pershing, smearing Dodi, the Captain
and Doron against the instrument panels.

Today fireworks explode between us and the camera.
No shells whine down; no one ducks; no one loses arms,
legs or life. We repeat that run again and again
because the spray of sand and dust obscures
the first takes.

This director doesn't know how the dried summer grass
caught fire from phosphor bullets whining overhead;
that we couldn't stand up to escape acrid flames
and had to roll from side to side puffing smoke, our eyes
watering the way smoldering fireplace logs ooze sap.

In our final scene, we jog along each side of the road,
machine guns swinging their legs against our boots.
The film crew doesn't know the way we clawed
shallow foxholes in that rocky hill, nor how we lay
with a view of the Golden Dome, shivering
through an unending night, our position exposed
in the glow of the Dormition Abbey flames. They omit
the mortar bombardment that churned dirt,
blinded Motti and pierced Sammi, the radioman.
They make no mention of the shell that found
Lieutenant Uri or how we carried him
to the medic station, in pieces.

After the shoot, we lie on our backs in the shade
of the scarred olive orchard, scoffing
at the camera crew and the notion of filming
a replay of war – anything to postpone going back
to the POW's and the prison of our memories.

YASSER'S WAR

Refuge

Homelessness: *statement of fact
or state of mind?*

Home could be a room –
even a bare room, in a camp, windowless.
Home is where you take a bloody nose
to have it wiped.

You drag yourself uphill,
hold back acrid tears
until they fall inside the doorway;
a bluster of late autumn rain
that fails to wash away pain.

Home is where your mail arrives.
When no one's there,
envelopes scatter on the floor.
They collapse in the entryway
like the wounded from a riot.

Home is where you go after a night
of running from the Security Police.
You search family faces for warm smiles,
a hiding place for grenades, a place of solace
for your bruised body and punctured pride.

You leave home to beg food, escape
a war, seek work, or join a fight.
You leave so often at night
the street feels more like home.

A bare room in a refugee camp
could be home. I, too, would devote
every minute and my life fighting
an army that blew up mine.

Bystander

*He who is present at a wrongdoing and does not lift
a hand to prevent it is as guilty as the wrongdoers.*

— American Omaha Indian Proverb

They beat him – I stood and watched.

Heavily armed, we marched through the village.
Some Green Berets caught one running away.
If he felt that guilty ... that was proof enough.
They pummeled him with clubs
near a well in the center square
inside a circle of tousled villagers,
within a cordon of watching soldiers
before five, in a fine morning mist.
To give the real culprits something
to think about, they beat him.

I watched and stood in silence.

He bled from his ears and when he fell, they kicked
his ribs. His children cried. His wife shrieked
for mercy, on her knees, arms outstretched.
They flung her aside like a dead cat.

In 1997, I read in a news report that the Israeli army
would withdraw from the West Bank.
An inquiry would be opened into the training
and methods of the green-bereted Border Police.

Too late for that Palestinian farmer
in ripped, blood-splattered pajamas.
Too late for me, still carrying
invisible scars all these years.

Dirge

Weep for my cousin Yasser,
killed by a Palestinian bomb
in his father's fields.

Cry for this severed sapling
struggling to root where he could
between wars and borders.

Wail for the youth of a people
whose history is a thousand years
of sacrificed heroes.

Grieve for this ten thousandth victim
of deceit, the majority of his life unlived;
this resister of repression and injustice

who found slingshot stones inadequate.
He let the *mullahs* strap a suicide belt
to his slender waist, press a trigger in his palm.

His aim: to earn eternal life
in his adolescent version of Islam's
heaven for killing Jews. Those same

Jews weep for the blood
drenching Yasser's father's fields;
property this son will never inherit.

Mourn this young martyr of the cause.
Mothers' tears wash blood
deep into the stony soil.

Khirbe

Cry for us all, for learning our lessons well.
Sentence me where you will, I've been to hell.
　　　　　　　　　　– The Trial, Lowell Jaeger, 1975

There was once a whole village here,
on a hill near Jerusalem.
Deir Yassin perched on hard layers
of pale limestone with rusty streaks,
quarried for building stones.

Villagers lived in dusty streets, houses
painted pastel blue and cream.
Boys with scuffed shoes played soccer
with a tin can. A squealing toddler
without clothes escaped from his mother.

Three donkeys loaded with cement sacks
struggled up the hill to a house
being built of white stone blocks.
Two hunched grandmothers hobbled past,
dressed in black from head to toe.

In the coffee shop beside the grocer's,
men on low stools played *sheshbesh*
but abandoned their bubbling *hookas*
and curling smoke when the *mouhezzin*
wailed the call to prayer from the minaret.

Today, the only sounds are the caw of a blackbird
on a mound of berry brambles
and the hollow spreet of sparrows.
One night in '48, the village vanished —
grandmothers and children, dogs and donkeys;
and later, the houses, shops and streets.

After twenty years, a place of silent hills
dotted with bleached limestone outcroppings,
like sheep grazing sparse green slopes.
It's a *khirbe*, a pile of bone-white stones, rimed
with lime, faint smears of pink; the chiseled edges
still visible through overgrown thorn bushes.

Neglected, abandoned and desolate,
you'd mistake it for a shepherd's cairn.

No other sign of man, Arab or Israeli,
no name, no marker, nor symbol on the map,
barely a blemish on anyone's conscience.

Wages of Innocence

In those days people will no longer say, "The fathers have eaten sour grapes, and the children's teeth are set on edge."
— Jeremiah 31:29

The Gaza shoemaker stitches soles on an ancient
foot-treadle sewing machine. The tiny shop, crammed
with dusty footwear, is wedged between a butcher's
and a leather merchant's. He never demonstrates;
doesn't even attend funerals. *I'm not political,* he says,
just trying to make a living. I wish harm to no one.

He spots the black curls of his dark-eyed son.
The six-year-old sits beneath the whirring machine,
making carts and sailboats from leather scraps.
Rukh. Go! Play outside. The boy goes to play,
sails his boats in the gutter.

The father patiently repairs peasants' shoes;
cutting, stitching, hammering on a last,
makes a rare pair for a rich patron
or a left shoe for a customer missing a leg.

Shouts from the street call to the shoemaker
to fetch his son, lying in the wet gutter
up the block amid pieces of leather.

Teenagers threw cobblestones.
Soldiers fired. The shoemaker runs.
A rubber bullet glancing off a lamppost
ripped though the child's thin throat.

The shoemaker wails; his face
contorted, the limp corpse of his son
draped across his blood-streaked arms.
He staggers blindly down the street.

Film clip of Arab carrying dead child
on street in Gaza on CNN.
Headlines at ten.

Embers

Look into my three-year-old's eyes
twinkling above her mouth,
moist with red pepperoni from my fingers.

The glow in her infant face pales
as you storm into the restaurant.
You shoulder explosive hatred
encrusted with screws and nails.
She hides her face in my chest.

You, who clutch the switch
in your clenched-tight fist,
your battle is with those
who dispossessed your father

or with Imams
who scarred your brain
with scourges of hell
and zeal of religion.

Look into my daughter's eyes
before you squeeze the trigger.
Know the fires of the future before
you try to quench them with your blood.

Black Birds

Lambs shelter from afternoon sun
in the shadows of the ewes. From the rocks
yellow eyes survey the honeyed meadow —
idyllic one minute, perfidious the next.

With drumming paws and bounds,
wolves focus their improvised explosion
on a luckless yearling. Iron teeth claw
the throat, wrench limb from shoulder.

Blood sprays, skin flies. The sated attackers
withdraw, trailing gore along the roadside.
Crows scavenge bits of flesh from gravel;
beaks peck tissue and sip blood.

Centuries-old religious law requires Jews
to bury corpses with all their body parts. On TV
after the bus bombing, black-clothed Burial Society
members gather scraps of flesh and shreds
of bloody cloth with tweezers and latex gloves.

Neither crow nor man waits for a post-mortem.
Neither stops the carnage.

Nevé Shalom – Paths of Peace

A response to Ada Aharoni, Israeli Peace Poet

Thirsty, I gulp your poems about Arab and Israeli
mothers marching in velvet, over rifts and chasms,
shepherding their children along a road to peace.

Nevé Shalom is appealing. My mind longs
to follow your pleasant paths but my heart,
my heart rebels, held hostage to the price.

Your *women's way* is too late for Dov. Despite
a childhood fever, he'd sued to enlist, to defend
against enemy legions. He waved to his daughters

as he marched off before Yom Kippur. He went
the soldiers' way, left one foot in the Suez sand,
the second in a pillar of fire atop Mt. Sinai.

Esther and the older children mourned.
The youngest never knew him. Now, as a teen,
she studies photos of a man in a family album.

I knew him, I tell her. *I loved him. A real peacenik,
he'd have given everything he owned for peace.
He'd say, "Give them back the land. Just stop the war."*

But when that everything included Dov, I fear
we paid too dearly. The word *Shalom* sticks
like shrapnel in my craw.

OTHERS' WARS

WW1 -- Glamorous War
(to a young man considering an army career)

> *And we are here as on a darkling plain*
> *Swept with confused alarms of struggle and flight,*
> *Where ignorant armies clash by night.*
> — *Dover Beach,* Matthew Arnold

You misled child, repeating glorious stories of brave
doughboys. You weren't told they were muddied
and bloodied, numbed with rum, and pushed
up from trenches like wheat from seed rows,
ripe for enemy scythes to slice to stubble.

Can't you see their blind faith was sanctified
with ignorance? They were ordered
to sacrifice themselves by beribboned
brass, posing as gods of war, quick
to squander other people's lives.

Before the "Good Fight" was the so-called
"War-To-End-All-Wars." It was a layer-cake
of ill-trained, ill-equipped youngsters like you,
buried in French rain-slicked mud. They
were sent off to war to bolster the claim
that those killed before had not died in vain.

Assault at Normandy

The drumming propellers
beat the water like a thousand horses
thundering. Waves tumble
over each other as they strain
to buoy up steel landing craft.

The breakers tremble and flee
outwards before the prow
slicing and slashing their backs.
With uneven rolling gait and foaming wakes,
boats force their way to the beach.
The battering offshore wind
can't slow their inexorable thrust.

But the soft cargo inside is easy prey.
Marines splash into the waves
from the stranded shells. A lurking current
sucks at their khaki leggings. The undertow
collaborates with the rapid fire from the shore.
The German bombardment pulverizes
and tints the surf pink.

Why is it Dark at Three O'Clock
and Why is Snow Falling?

Where are these girls and boys, women and men going?
Why do they carry small suitcases?
Why would people, not in uniform, walk in a column?
Are they going to the train station?
Why do they crowd into cattle wagons?
Why don't they travel on passenger trains?
Where are these trains going?
Can mothers and fathers and children travel together?
What will happen when they get there?
If they are separated, will the little ones cry?
How will they ever find each other again?
How can the trains take a whole race?
Will the trains bring them back?

Poem with

25   Random Numbers

At Gallipoli
          in February 1915,
          in the first
2   beachheads, the Allies landed
2,000   men, and
95%   were killed or wounded.
          Things got worse after that.
1,000,000   troops from both sides fought
          on the peninsula. In December,
          the "successful" Allied retreat
          evacuated the last
140,000   men from the beaches. Dead
          and wounded totaled
630,000   men. Averaged over those
10   months, this is more than
2,000   men a day. That was only
          a small part of WWI.

In all of
WW I,   called the War-to-End-All-Wars
61,000,000   soldiers fought for 4 years, during which
37,000,000   were killed, wounded, captured,
          or missing, and another 22% or
8,000,000   civilians were killed. Not counting the
21,000,000   who died in the 1918 Influenza Pandemic,
          this averages to
31,000   per day – mothers & fathers, brothers
          & sisters, daughters & sons
          and some days were worse.

Compare   that to
WWII   we (people) killed or wounded
77,000,000   human beings. Almost 50% were civilians,
          not even armed.
77,000,000   people averages over 6 years to about
35,000   per day.
          We were more advanced by then.

Nailbiter

1. Mr. Cortes taught us Shakespeare.
   He stuttered through Macbeth,
   chewed his thumbnail through Hamlet
   until only a deformed stub remained.

   He blamed it all on shell-shock,
   the battles near Anzio; 18-year-olds
   plunging into bleeding waves
   between floating bodies of Aussies
   and Kiwis in '42, before we were born.

   His Highlanders' attack on Chiusi
   was the reason for his large belly, he said, soldiers
   eating when food was available; his insomnia
   the result of interrupted sleep; his jitters
   and stammer caused by the bombardments.

   We mimicked his speech, mocked
   the 45-year-old belly that hung over his belt,
   the label of his slacks flipped outwards,
   the wrinkled trousers and the shine
   on his pants' seat. None of us asked about his War.

2. We should have.
          We should have before
   we found ourselves knee-deep in our own Chiusi,
   cutting through barbed wire, weaving past mines,
   dodging shells and shrapnel,

   crawling face-down between bodies
   and staccato bursts of gun fire.
   We learned how hard it is to live with
   ghosts of slain friends, memories and regrets.

   Only then, too late, did we understand Cortes,
   his nightmares and daydreams, torn between
   thoughtless students and his need to beg
   forgiveness for surviving.

Saffron Sage

For Stu

The captain and the monk
sit in front of an orphanage.
Khaki and saffron talk of tea,
ponder faith, fish and food,
discuss ceremony versus style
on the shore of a yellow sea.

They eat red and green rice
carried by the VC down the HCM Trail,
dodging gunships' *Sturm* and napalm *Drang*,
jumping from foxhole to crater
in woven reed hats, portering rice
to honor *Tet* Festival guests.

The Buddhist monk talks of not having
nor wanting more than he has.
The polite American captain hankers after
US-of-A hot dogs, his girlfriend and Chevrolet.

They sit and talk, and on the shore
the greenback whale lies beached
and helicopters slice through
the tortured sky over an ocean of blood.

Phone Call

Saigon, April 1975

Women shriek, soldiers yell, men wail.
The chained Embassy gates sway and bend
under the panic of the massed bodies.
Overhead, incessant flap-flapping
of chopper blades plucks the lucky from the roof.

At the fence, mothers offer the Marines their infants
swaddled in jewelry, "Take my child. Save my baby!"

The rotor downdraft from each Air America
lift-off buffets the frail hopes of the waiting mob.

All day long, fathers, mothers, children, girlfriends
clamor, scratch and claw. They jam their faces
between the iron bars, scream and screech
above the motors' roar, beg to be saved.

Inside the Embassy, we're busy
shredding reports and burning secrets.
A buddy of mine is called to the phone.

For a year, he and I dated two local waitresses,
Le Ly and Mai. I hadn't heard from Mai in months.

He returns from his call, ashen-faced, shaking.
It was Le Ly, crying to be taken with him to the States.

When he tells her he can't, she kills herself.
He hears the gunshot over the phone.

Before the end, he stammers in tears, she tells him
my girl, Mai, gave birth to a son.

The next phone call's for me.

Based on a 1977 interview with ex-CIA Officer Frank Snepp, author of
the book *Decent Interval.*

Shame

The National Security Agency (NSA) has a list of Iraq-war protesters. President Bush says the list is legal.
— *New York Times,* December 16, 2005

I'm ashamed; but not of my President.

I work in an office, follow my daily routine
like a religious mantra. I buy Christmas gifts,
choose between tournedos and salmon
in a French restaurant, and read the news.

In this quiet town, seagulls break
the silence; there are few competing
sirens, no fighter jets; the nights are lit
by a flaccid moon, not explosions.

I'm ashamed – but not of my country.

I abhor the randomness of gunfire,
decry indiscriminate bombings,
execrate extremist violence.
I know this war is wrongly pursued,

its *raison d'etre,* to sow death
misguided, encouraged by unfocused
revenge and greed. I crave peace.
I'm ashamed; but not of the NSA.

I'm ashamed I didn't stand up, thunder
parables like Nathan to King David; shout out,
demanding change like Jeremiah.
I'm ashamed of myself –
my name is not on that list.

On the Road to Tehran

or really, on a dusty shoulder, leading east
from Ba'qubah, he sits drinking tepid water
from a bottle, sweating in a plush blue armchair
taken from the house near the checkpoint.

Every day, sun, dust, and children's taunts, MREs,
interrupted sleep. No infiltrators, no WMDs; but each
unlucky farmer that passes is searched. The tension
wears on; monotony punctuated by distant bombs.

Finally, a report of an insurgent hiding in the house
near the checkpoint. "Take out Abu-Saeed;
he's a bomb maker." Sounds reasonable: ties in with
traffic, packages, averted eyes.

Reinforcements surround the house, weapons
readied. He hammers on the door with his rifle butt,
then kicks it in. Yelling soldiers flood the house.
In the living room, a man sits on the tile floor,
watching TV. Children flee to the women's room.

"Abu-Saeed?"
>> *No, No!* shaking head. In his pajamas, he jumps up,
>> nervous hands held high, clutching papers.
"Where is Abu-Saeed?"
>> *I not know – gone.*
"We need the bomb maker."
>> *Please. He gone.*
"You'll do."

The soldier yanks him outside; shoots him in the head.

Based on a Reuters news report, January 2007.
One U.S. soldier was tried for murder.

Meat on Butcher Street

A dull explosion.
A boy with electric eyes and wild hair dashes through
the *Suq*, where alleys criss-cross the warren
under stone arches, along rows of small shops.
He dodges between bushels of green fava beans,
leaps over piled sacks of white barley.

The smells of each street advertise the merchandise.
Hawkers call out their wares, strain for attention
of milling crowds, drowned out by clatter of donkeys'
hooves on the cobbled alleys, their sagging backs
saddled with panniers of corn and bags of cement.

Curry, coriander, and cardamom thicken the air.
The piles of spices, animals, throngs of shoppers swirl
in a turbulence of earthy tones, scents and voices.

The boy glances back, stalled behind a slow woman.
Sandaled feet poke out below the hem of her black robes.

The air turns from spices to tannery leather. On the store
fronts hang bridles and saddles. A shoemaker sits tapping
nails into a sole on a last between his knees.

The boy swerves away from the shriek of a grind wheel
spewing sparks on Metal Merchants Street, glances
over his shoulder again for signs of round helmets,
then plunges ahead into the cloying odor of raw meat.

A skinned lamb with pink-gray muscles obscenely
exposed, live chickens, a quartered cow,
looped intestines, on hooks on the walls. Buzzing

clouds of flies are shooed by a child waving
a horsehair whisk. The butcher balances
a small, notched stick, hung in the middle
from a loop of string. On one end dangles
a brass pan with assorted weights.

From a hook on the other, hangs
a thick beef tongue. A customer stands,
bargains at the top of her voice.

The boy with electric eyes
pushes headlong into the shop,
through customers and chickens.
Feathers fly, wings thrash.
The butcher turns abruptly,
surges after the boy into the back.

They hide between hanging slabs
of beef. The older man slips the boy
into a rope harness and wordlessly
lifts him by his knees. The boy flings
a loop over a hook and swings,
pressed in on all sides by carcasses.

The butcher hurries to the front.
His customers have vanished.
The shop is deserted. He looks
down at his shaking hands.
Military boots resound,
clomping on cobbles.

Uniformed, helmeted soldiers
guns slung from their shoulders,
push through crowds. They stop
in the suddenly still street
in front of the butcher shop.

Not Family

For Steve

We fly to Ramadi City to supervise the new
Theater Internment Facility with 130
of the 13,000 detainees headed for new prisons.
We watch the rows of prisoners, blindfolded,
shackled to each other, hand and foot,
stumbling into a C-150's cavernous belly.

All wear yellow prison tee shirts and pants.
Some pose defiantly, heads held high.
Others look away. All are young, rounded up
for some reason, suspect by action or association,
except

one crumpled and folded old man, balding
and wrinkled, notable because of his age. He, too,
shuffles into the maw of the craft. Soldiers follow,
sitting on the ramp as it's drawn up, sealing them
into the dark shell of the plane.

Soldiers and prisoners sit or lie
on the vibrating floor as the plane rumbles down
the runway, lifts off and goes through gyrations,
sudden drops and turns to evade possible rocket fire.
Even the seasoned fliers among the soldiers

use the vomit bags from their field first aid kits.
The detainees sit shoulder to shoulder
on rolls of plastic in case they soil themselves,
one way or another.

A month later, two majors and I
sit on a review board to screen detainees,
evaluate the threat level they pose.
The dossiers describe why each man
was apprehended. Then we let them talk.
The English of the translator is broken.
Some of them scream invective at the US, some

are innocent, others were turned in by enemies.
All claim they should be released.
Until the bent old man is ushered in.
He'd been taken from a house where
a sheikh, the political enemy
of a local bigwig, was arrested.

This man's only crime:
wrong place, wrong time.
We confer, decide to release him.
He stands and speaks. Tears
fall, darkening the yellow shirt.

Translator:
Mister Major, why you send me back?
To home? What home? To family? What family?
My home is exploded by fighters who say
I with Amrika. My wife, my girls
in camp for refugees; no man, no food,
no money. My son run away – gone.
I no have home, not family, not anything.

Another Monument to War

The • shiny • black • marble, • carved • with • your • names • retreat. • Polished • g
You • who • wouldn't, • couldn't, didn't • back • ou
noms • de • guerre • drops • to • a • nadir, • like • an • arrowhead • po
somber • and • reflective • memorial • stands • as • a • resting • plac
thousand • of • you, • sent • half • way • 'round • the • world • to • die, •
develop • a • defoliant, • bolster • an • ego • or • finish • some • foreig
war. • The • gleaming • basalt • is • a • message • to • you: • "Your •
deaths • were • not • in • vain. • We • strive • to • honor •
and • admire • you, • just • not • enough • to •
hold • you • safe • from • another •
pointless • war."

ts • into • the • ear th • as • deep • as • you • are • buried. •
abbro-basalt•wa ll • graffitied • wit h • your •
inting•to•the•fa ding • past. • The •
e•in•time,•for•fi fty • eight •
to•end•a•recess ion, •
ners' • dirty •

Nice Guys

For Kelly

Joe was his name. We met in Fort Bragg, '64,
real nice guy. I heard he went down in a chopper.
Joe Tallon – must have been thirty.
He got me out of a mess. Saved my ass.
Afterwards, we talked some.
He had parents in Hawaii
and a girlfriend in Trinidad.
They were going to get married,
but I heard he went down in a chopper.
Can't find his name on the Wall.
Talley – Tallion – Tallman – nope.
Could I be wrong? Could he have made it?
Maybe it was T-a-l-a-n?
Aw, shit! There it is – Ariston R. Talan.
That's right. But we called him Joe.
That's him, Ariston Talan.
A real nice guy.

Del was younger. Said he had a kid. Just a kid himself.
Del Lefleme, La-flam he pronounced it.
Probably some French in his blood,
but he was from Salem, Oregon.
His unit ambushed his first week in 'Nam.
Can't see Lefleme. Look for Del, no, Delbert,
his full name; was shy about it too.
Look at all the Delberts! Delbert
Leasure ... Lewis ... La Flemme,
Delbert Charles. That's him.
Delbert Charles La Flemme. Just a kid.
His first week in 'Nam.

Real nice guys. Every one of 'em.

You Don't Know Scared

Why did you leave Afghanistan in 1990?

We run away; scared.

All soldiers are scared in war, but they
control their fear. Just suck it up.

You don't know "scared."

What d'ya mean?

I am lookout on roof on Army barracks. I have good view, all sides, yes? You think they have good view of me also? You are right. But they don't shoot to me. No. Instead they put Yuri in street, near barracks, enough near to hear Yuri calling loud, "Help me, Comrades! For love of God, I begging of you, help me." You understand? No one go to help Yuri. I, myself even, lie still, and Yuri is my closest – how you say, "buddy." An hour he is crying those words, his voice growing lower and slower. Then he say, "Stefan." Stefan – my name. Yuri knows sniper position on the roof. Three nights ago, he and me, we lie there, together – lookout duty. "Stefan," now he is crying quietly, "Stefan, in the name of our friendship, in the name of everyone you love, Stefan, shoot me!" I cry too. My eyes sting. I don't know anything to do. I am very scared.

You see, two nights before, when we go patrol in Kabul, there is a shooting attack. Yuri gets lost. Disappear. We scared he is prisoner. The mujahid Hekmatyar -- his Hezb-e-Islami terrorists find Yuri. We know this true now, because Yuri he is lying without clothes, dying in street. We can see what these peoples cut his stomach and down from that. His feet are broken, his hands are chopped and wrists tight with wires to slow blood coming out. He has other parts missing. Blood around him, slowly there is more, turn black in sand between mud buildings. On his chest, big package. Yellow plastics tied with tapes and with explosion wire. You touch him – boom!

It happen with Xander, with Agrimov, and others like that before. One day before, Agrimov run to help his brother Xander, when he is same like Yuri. Xander, Agrimov, houses, all blow up; make big hole, big bang.

No. You don't know "scared" like this.

Kandahar Haiku

Playing in minefields
Afghan boys can't imagine
Their youth undamaged

Grandpa Cries

Homo homini lupus est
(man is a wolf towards man)
                    — Plautus

Ma says his doctor said Grandpa cries
'cause he's old and his hormonies are upset –
not from anything I done – something in his old blood
pushes tears out his tired eyes.

I told him I'm almost eight and I don't cry all the time,
not any more. Grandpa says homo hominy lupins' nest –
but my teacher said not to say that word.
Grandpa says I should ask my Miss Hart how many
Russkies, Gypsies and Chews died from Germs and Stallin'.

Ma says Pa stop it. Grandpa says one day I'll learn
about the Chaps wiping out Chinese, about Truks
and Amen-ians, and Orange men and about
Cat-licks in Eyeland. That's names of dead people,
millions of 'em.

Ma says it's because he's old.
Grandpa says it's you men history.
I think he's prob'ly right to cry
about fightin' and dyin'.

Mount Timpanogos Talks

Your ways and your deeds
have done this to you;
this is your wickedness,
how bitter it is,
how it has touched your heart.
　　　　　　　　　— Jeremiah, 4:18

"Pay attention," said old Timpanogos
in a biblical boom, during a recent storm.
"The difference between mountains

and men is: you use emotions to keep things up.
We have our tectonic uplifts. But everyone
and everything is within the pull of gravity.

Mountains wear down grain by grain.
Men level each other with bombs,
guns, sticks and stones, poison and plagues.

Mountains have learned that we either
stick together or fall apart. But you tear
each other down – make gravity's job easy.

Nature tries to clean up your mess but
everything has its limit. Man must change.

Jeremiah had it right,
even though he's one of you."

Desert Dreamer

I escape scheming politicians,
and the welter of war. I leave crowds
of panicked, pushing city people
to follow previous recluses along dusty
unpaved paths into the white-hot *Aravah,*
the arid Rift Valley south of the Dead Sea.

The bone-dry air shimmers, towering walls
of layered rock sway like belly dancers.
Eons ago, a huge rent opened here,
leaving interrupted strata hanging
on parched palisades on each side.
The far flank is lost in blinding glare.

Landslide-tumbled rocks pile
in castled ruins. I see only precipices,
sand and bleached sky. Thirsty, alone,
I walk with silence; silence so loud I can
hear ghosts dancing on the fiery
rocks, whispering, Hot.

I feel like Moses, barefoot before
a burning bush in a waterless desert.
Then I cease to be – no body, no thoughts,
no desert cliffs, no heat, no war. Quiet,
floating, silent. A shadow passes.

I think: vulture. I squint in the brilliance.
A sand-colored desert lark flutters
above my head; in its beak – green life.
Its whirring wings cool my cheek,
whispering to the world in mother tongues,
sperare, espérer, esperanza – hope.

On the Lawn of the War Memorial

For Juan Carlos

WWII artillery pieces point north and west. A flagpole stands quietly at attention amid the smell of mown grass and eucalyptol. Thin-fingered gum trees wave their leaves above scattered picnickers sprawled on rugs. A Frisbee hovers in the bright blue overhead, an orange flying saucer. It sinks toward a tall scraggle-bearded teenager like a golden plastic sunhat. He snatches it out of the warm air as it floats by. There's a smile on his lips when he tries it on his head, then whirls it to the top of a eucalyptus. Tangled in the mottled bark of the branches, the straw-colored plastic pauses, then flutters to the grass. An elderly grandmother clutches it, now a rough woven straw hat with floppy gray brim, to her chest. With delight and a surprising stride, she flicks it skyward. It spins, soars and sails on the light wind, dips and dives, straight into my hands. The loose straw weave feels unexpectedly soft in my fingers and palms. As I cradle it like a bowl, the floppy brim folds downwards and folds again, until the round shape is a small pulsing bindle with a throbbing heart like a kitten perhaps, moving and warm. As I open my fingers, the tawny shape filigrees to feathers; an auburn-breasted robin unfurls gray wings, pushes my hands apart, and flaps its way to the treetops to disappear in sun and light.

Immortal Enough

People play hide-and-seek with the Angel
of Death all their lives. When they get close
to losing, they hide from view.

Some seek solace in a life hereafter.
Not me.

I need nothing after life. One's enough.
I'll happily feed the worms, bacteria,
scavengers, and plants.

My next life is in cedars and pines,
sailfish and seagulls, in the bodies
and voices of children ignorant of death.

I'll live in a newborn's cry, a toddler's first steps,
in the breath used to say "Mama" and "Baba,"
in his first word read aloud, his small finger
touching the page, in her first "A"
penciled on lined paper.

I'll live in their first falling in love – forever.

Daisies in Rifle Barrels

Alliant Technology, Inc. announces an increase of 17% in third quarter orders, raising revenues to $900 million, as war boosts the demand for bullets.

— *Reuters*, January 26, 2007

At the Kent State protest in 1970, we
were naïve, didn't know that a bullet
could spew from a rifle barrel fast
as a jet, destroy daisies, kill daughters and sons.

We didn't know that armies could be marched
into ambush, that despots lie, that greed corrupts
and ambition could be classified as National Security;
that a thousand mothers could birth, breast-feed,
wean, and raise a thousand disposable soldiers
to be called collateral damage, gambled on a losing bet.

We didn't know that every rifle bullet manufactured
for the army is intended for some mother's child.

But, by God, we do now.

OTHER INFORMATION

Author Biography

Jon Sebba was born in South Africa. After high school, he lived in Israel for eight years. There he studied geology among other things. As a student in Jerusalem, he worked cataloging 19th Century medical journals, as well as at the Hydrology Institute. He also worked as a laborer in the construction of Jerusalem apartment buildings and of evaporation lagoons at the Dead Sea (1400 feet below sea level) with summer temperatures topping 115°F.

When the 1967 Arab-Israeli Six Day War began, he was married with one child. As a reservist, he was mobilized to fight in Jerusalem. Among the things he learned from that experience are: death in war is random; wars should definitely be avoided; and given the choice, few soldiers would ever start one.

In 1968, Jon immigrated to the US to study civil engineering, arriving the day before Rev. Martin Luther King was assassinated. En route, he worked as a lorry driver in London for four months. He has lived and worked as an engineer in six states, divorced and remarried. He now lives in Murray, Utah, with his wife and muse, Chris. Together they have four children scattered across the US.

Jon has been writing poetry since the 1970's. In early 2013, he had a play produced at the Gallery Theater in Ogden. He has written a movie script and is currently writing a novel. Both stories are based on the lives of people he knew growing up under apartheid in Cape Town.

Almost six years ago, Chris and Jon were presented with a grandson – a gift which has changed their lives. Thanks to Declan, they feel encouraged about the future.

Jon can be reached at yossi.yasser.soldiers@gmail.com.

Previous Utah Poets of the Year

1965 - Vesta P. Crawford, *Short Grass Woman*
1966 - Lael W. Hill, *A Legacy of Years*
1967 - Berta H. Christensen, *Walk the Proud Morning*
1968 - Betty W. Madsen, *The Amaranth*
1969 - J. A. Christensen, *The Deep Song*
1970 - Max Golightly, *A Morning of Taurus*
1971 - Alice Morrey Bailey, *Eden from an Apple Seed*
1972 - Maxine R. Jennings, *A Lamp to Shine*
1973 - Geraldine R. Pratt, *Bell on the Wind*
1974 - LeRoy Burke Meagher, *Beyond This Hour*
1975 - Helen Mar Cook, *Shape of Flight*
1976 - Caroline Eyring Miner, *Lasso the Sunrise*
1977 - Clarence P. Socwell, *Intrinsic Tapestries*
1978 - Pearle M. Olsen, *Frame the Lace Moments*
1979 - Randall L. Hall, *Mosaic*
1980 - La Verde Morgan Clayson, *Furrows of Renewal*
1981 - Frank M. DeCaria, *Songs Within the Sounds*
1982 - LaVon B. Carroll, *The Shrouded Carousel*
1983 - Bonnie Howe Behunin, *Wake the Unicorn*
1984 - Joyce Ellen Davis, *In Willy's House*
1985 - Patricia S. Grimm, *Timepiece*
1986 - Dorothy Logan, *Child in a Sculptured Bowl*
1987 - Kathryn Clement, *Riddlestone*
1988 - Sherwin W. Howard, *Sometime Voices*
1989 - Maryan Paxton, *Downwind Toward Night*
1990 - Elaine Christensen, *At the Edges*
1991 - Robert J. Frederickson, *Being Here*
1992 - Brad Roghaar, *Unraveling the Knot*
1993 - Margaret Pettis, *Chokecherry Rain*
1994 - Muriel Heal Bywater, *Stretching Toward Wild Swans*
1995 - Elaine Ipson, *Where Ghosts are Garrisoned*
1996 - Nancy Hanks Baird, *The Shell in Silk*
1997 - Marilyn Darley Williams, *The Red Rooster Cafe*
1998 - Mikal Lofgren, *Trudi Smiles Back*
1999 - Marilyn Bushman-Carlton, *Cheat Grass*
2000 - Kolette Montague, *Easing Into Light*
2001 - Rita Bowles, *God in Assorted Boxes*
2002 - Evelyn Hughes, *Furnace of Affliction*
2003 - Judy Johns, *If I Could Speak in Silk*

2004 - Maurine Haltiner, *A Season and a Time*
2005 - T. Kevin Clark, *Song of an Oquirrh Son*
2006 - Sue Ranglack, *Shouting from the Book of Orange*
2007 - N. Colwell Snell, *Hand Me My Shadow*
2008 - Helen Keith Beaman, *Edges Disappear*
2009 - Gail G. Schimmelpfennig, *The Frozen Kingdom*
2010 – Rosalyn Whitaker Ostler, *Walking the Earth Barefoot*
2011 – Lee C. Snell, *Night Wind Home*
2012 – Dawnell H. Griffin, *On Judgment Day*

Prior Publication and Awards

The poem *"Nevé Shalom – Paths of Peace"* was first published in about 1980 in Voices-Israel, a periodical of English poetry printed in Israel.

A version of "Forty-Five and Counting" won First Place in the Zara Sabin Memorial Category, UTSPS, 1999.

"Phone Call" was awarded 1st Place in the Dale Cutting Social and Political Issues Category, UTSPS, 2001.

"Daisies in Rifle Barrels" earned 3rd Place in the Zara Sabin Memorial Category, UTSPS, 2008

Utah State Poetry Society Book Publication Award

In 1965, Nicholas Morgan and Paul Pehrson established a revolving fund to publish a book by the person whom the Utah State Poetry Society, following a statewide contest, designated Utah Poet of the Year. As costs increased, UTSPS assisted by the Utah Arts Council, supplemented the fund. In 1985, Pearle M. Olsen, the 1978 recipient, donated a large sum to assist the project. Subsequently, Mrs. Olsen's children John K. M. Olsen, Billye O. Jenkins, and Carlyle O. Morris, made further contributions to ensure continuation of the project.

In 2011, substantial donations to the Poetry Society from the Johnson Family, the Hanks Family and other friends allowed this well-loved project to continue. The name was changed to the Utah State Poetry Society Book Publication Award to reflect this new sponsorship.

Yossi, Yasser, and Other Soldiers by Jon Sebba is the forty-ninth volume in this valuable series.